Black River Art

Presents

Fifty Fun Fur Babies

This Book Belongs To

_____

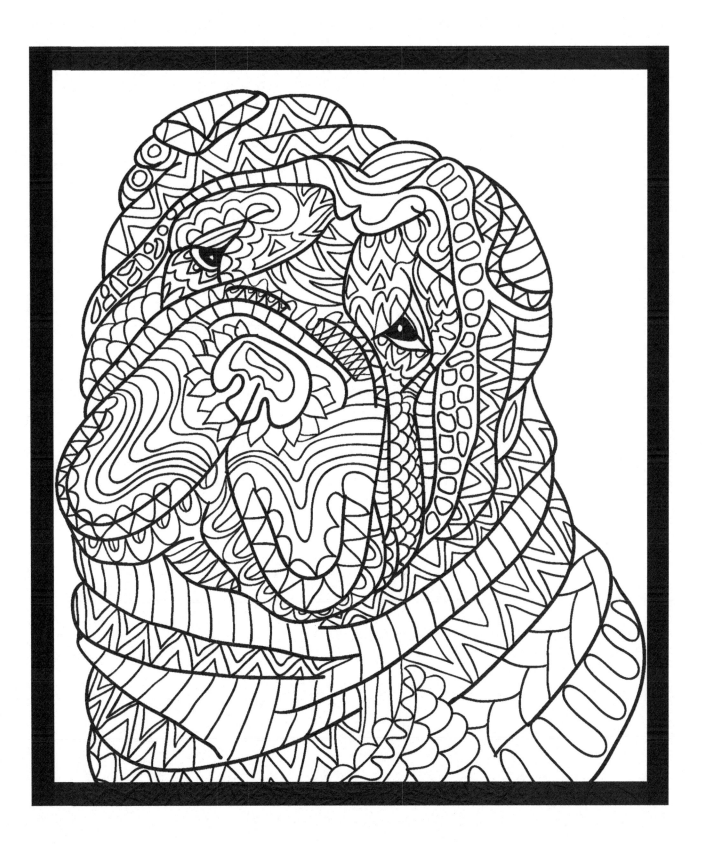

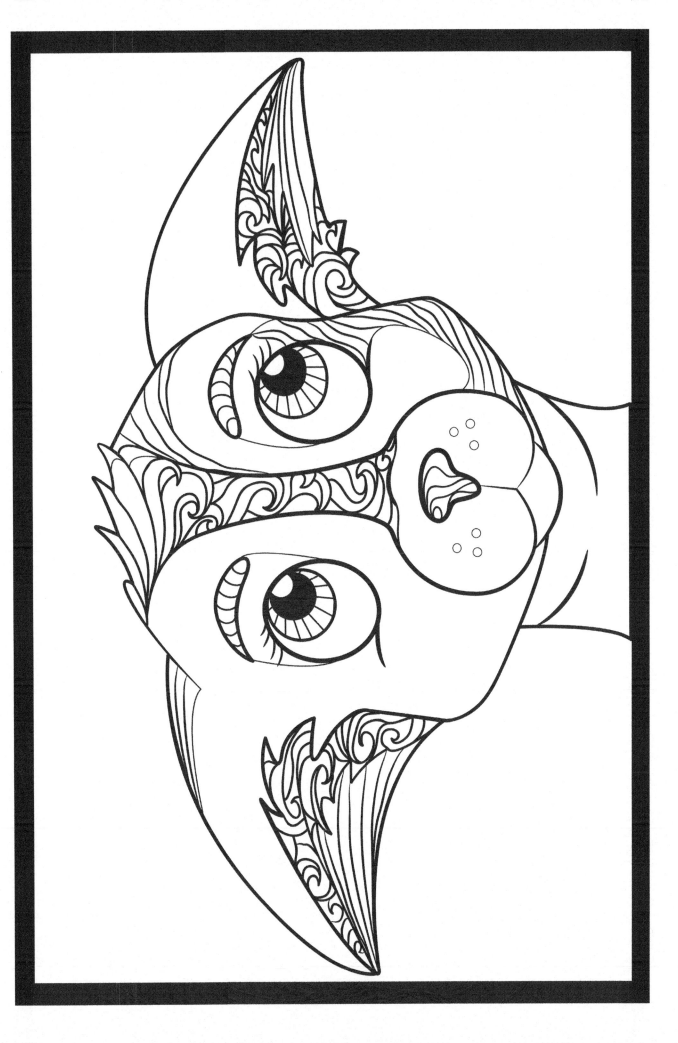

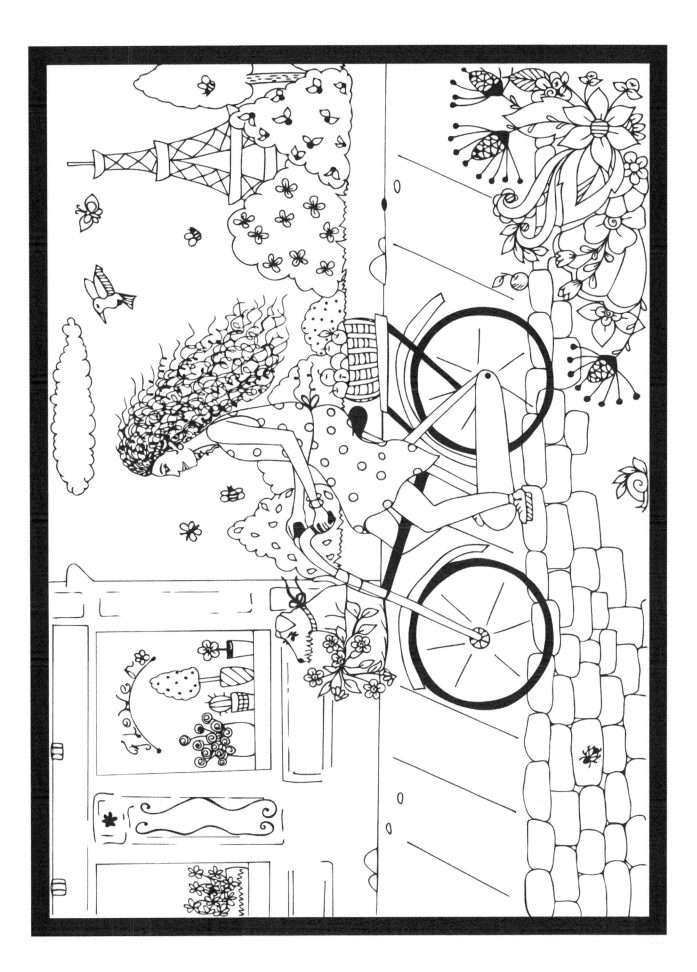

Other Titles Available

Fifty Fun Felines

Color Some Whimsy

Life is Good

Coloring on the Edge Halloween

Coloring Doodlez

My Big Fat Coloring Book

Color Some Cuteness

Oodles of Animals

Check out our travel size
coloring books too.

Made in the USA
Las Vegas, NV
17 February 2022